The Underside of Light

For Jane —
a dear friend and wonderful
writer.

The Underside of Light

Blessings,

Wayne Lee

9-19-14
Hillsboro, OR

Aldrich Press

Cover photograph: Wayne Lee

ISBN: 13: 978-0615878997

Aldrich Press
24600 Mountain Avenue, 35
Hemet, California 92544

for Alice —
my partner, friend, lover, editor, collaborator & wife

Acknowledgements

My thanks to the editors of the publications where the following poems previously appeared, sometimes in alternate versions:

Adobe Walls: "Wolf Moon"; *Aunt Chloe:* "Back When I Used to be White" & "Song for Rahim Alhaj"; *Barranca Press:* "Sha-Sha Says"; *Clapboard House* (online): "Home Before Dark" & "Bottle Tree"; *Collecting Life: Poets on Objects Known and Imagined:* "White Glass"; *Conversations Across Borders* (online): "Play of Light"; *Fixed & Free:* "Carrizozo Waitress"; *How to....Multiple Perspectives on Creating a Garden, a Life, Relationships and Community:* "Squash Bugs," "Seed Pot," "Planting in May" & "Flicker in the Cottonwood"; *Lowestoft Chronicle:* "Ordinary Deckhand"; *Lucidity Poetry Journal:* "Trial by Canoe"; *Malpais Review:* "Sections," "Truckstop Theory" & "Ingénue"; *Manorborn:* "Swimming Through Space"; *Mas Téquila Review:* "A Face in the Ice" & "Carrizozo Waitress"; *New Mexico Poetry Review:* "High Desert Monsoon", "The Human Scale" & "Thirst"; *New Millennium:* "My Father's War"; *Quill & Parchment:* "High Desert Monsoon"; *Sage Trail Poetry Magazine:* "Evening Prayer"; *Santa Fe New Mexican:* "Artificial Tree"; *Santa Fe Literary Review*: "Placenta"; *The Santa Fe Reporter:* "My Father's War"; *Steam Ticket:* "A Face in the Ice"; *Tupelo Press Poetry Project* (online): "The one with violets in her lap"; *Voices Israel* (online): "The Fortieth Day."

"Cold Mountain" was the SICA Poems for Peace Prize winner.
"My Father's War" was a *Santa Fe Reporter* War and Peace
    Poetry Contest winner.
"Ordinary Deckhand" was nominated for a Pushcart Prize.

Thanks also to the following:

My family, for their love & support: Mom, Sheryl, Don, Jim, Shelley, Molly, Mica, Johannes, & Annie; My friends & colleagues, for their guidance & critical contributions: Donald Levering, Barbara Rockman, Sheila Cowing, Robyn Hunt, Gary Worth Moody, Mary Morris, David Marquardt, Susan Gardner, Devon Ross, Michael Scofield, Paul White, Billy Brown, Kenneth Gurney, James McGrath, Rachelle Woods, Jim & Elizabeth Raby, Carl Phillips, Erin Belieu, Cate Marvin, Jordan Hartt, Sandi Sartorelli, Knute Skinner, Robert Huff, Viola Weinberg, James Bertolino, Anita Boyle, Jane Allyn, Steven Roxborough, Susan J. Erickson & Steven Dolmatz; and finally, my editor, Karen Kelsay.

What Other Poets are Saying

I cannot tell you when I've read a collection of poems that moved me as much as this one. The poetry makes imaginative leaps into other places, other times, and other lives. Despite, or because of, his "history of grief," Lee's poetry is witty, sometimes laughter-provoking, and always marked by a generous humanity. Lee has "learned from experts how to mediate anarchy loosed upon the world" and to take pleasure in the quotidian, ants, dogs, flannel sheets. "At this point, we can't be picky, / we'll take what weather we are sent— / a morning in the sun, / an afternoon of turbulent white, / preparation for the night." *The Underside of Light* reminds us that compassion still exists.

~ Elizabeth Raby, author of *Ink on Snow* and *This Woman*

With a linguistic elegance that approaches dance, Wayne Lee gifts the reader with a finely honed edge on which balances music and image, compelling each of us to witness, beyond species or gender, *The Underside of Light*, in which our most private and public emotions become illuminant, drawing us inexorably toward the flame of our shared humanity.

~ Gary Worth Moody, author of *Hazards of Grace* and *Occaquan*

To see through another's eyes, read their poetry. Wayne Lee's vision is 20/20. I now see what had become common from a new angle that reignites interest. I expanded my wealth of experiences through *The Underside of Light*.

~ Kenneth P. Gurney, author of *Curvature of a Fluid Spine,* and editor of *Adobe Walls*

"What is to give light must endure burning."

— *Viktor Frankl (1905-1977)*

Table of Contents

III.

I.

Ordinary Deckhand

With zen mind, beginner's mind,
let me pretend I've never sailed this sound
so I can see these breaching whales

with newfound eyes, adolescent eyes,
hear these bells and horns, these
glaucous gulls, with novice ears,

smell this giant kelp and ocean salt,
this diesel smoke with nostrils open to the fog,
let me forget I ever steered these straights,

rode these riptides, charted this course,
let me unlearn how to coil that rope,
scrub that hold, pump that bilge,

gut that sockeye salmon and halibut,
with wild mind, child's mind,
let me un-identify these harbor lights

and no-name points, un-navigate
that bay and channel, bank and rock,
not drop anchor in these hidden coves,

with pure heart, perfect heart,
let me restart the engine of my imagination
and abandon all my new-formed memories

like cork floats washed ashore
on nameless reefs and untamed shoals
and wake my ordinary deckhand soul.

More Than Darkness

Today Sensei asked us to stare
at an object
for half an hour.

I watched my eyelids.

Not to shut out sight, not
to sleep.

More than darkness there:
pattern,
pulse,

memory: The underside of light.

The only part of myself
I cannot see, not
even with reflection.

The opposite of a flounder:

Sections

I peel an orange to give it away.
Such sour and sweetness in one skin.
(How many sections does one orange have?)

I place a piece on a rock in the woods
as tithing for coyotes and owls
(such sour and sweetness in one skin.)

I proffer a portion to the postman
(I peel an orange to give it away)
mail another to our daughter in Berlin.

One goes into the offering plate
(how many sections does one orange have?)
our dog steals two off the kitchen counter.

I plant another by the sour cherry tree
(such sweetness!), leave one for a mendicant.
How many sections do I give away?

The Skins of Vegetables

— after Virginia Woolf (1882-1941)

This is what she was thinking (the uselessness,
the waste, utility discarded like a placenta) as
she peeled first the potato (the lowly laborer,
never too proud for menial duty), then the beet
(its regal root cousin), and the carrot (in gaudy
striptease, almost aglow), then lopped the
stalk (if that is what it is called) of broccoli,
whose lost, succulent heart constitutes perhaps
the saddest misuse of all — for, in our haste,
she concluded, stepping to the window to
watch the ominous accumulation of cumulus
(even while expecting the dawn to blush like
a radish), to extract the very core of something
(essence, zest, love) we (all of us, don't we?)
toss the rootstock (the future, in fact) out with
the rinsewater, at which point (despite the
rising panic of willow, the stoic oak) she
turned again toward the cornucopia that would
sustain them (even as the storm approached;
cows knelt in alfalfa; field mice fled for
woodsheds), toward yet another supper,
another sleep, (in which again she kicks off
the bedcovers), another awakening, naked
and starved.

Vortex

They arrive in waves just before dusk,
swarm and swirl over marshes and mudflats
along the lower Connecticut River half a mile
from Long Island Sound — hundreds
of thousands of common tree swallows —
migrating from miles around, converging
in a vortex thick as gnats, suddenly
plummeting to earth and vanishing
into a pond-sized patch of twelve-foot reeds.

My young friend Evelyn complained
of headaches, was diagnosed with stage three
cancer of the brain that surgery failed to extricate,
her tumor now bombarded both by chemo
and radiation so-called therapies —
Evelyn at thirty-seven watching helpless
as the spin of her life winds down. I want

those swallows to aim the funnel cloud
of their calling like an ion beam
at Evelyn's aching skull, to make her sickness
dissipate into the dying light. I want to hide her
in a thicket of cattails and saw-grass,
shield her from the predatory sky.

Like frightened birds, I share the drive to dive
for camouflage — at least for this one night —
at least until I know I'm safe from peregrine falcon
and sharp shinned hawk, free of malignancies,
hidden from forces I cannot see.

The Fortieth Day

An angel rises
from thunderheads erupting
over mountains.

Be aware, the messenger implores.
Although you haven't had rain
in forty days,

that could change in one afternoon.
Be alert, watch for movement
among the juniper.

This is where you saw the coyote
on your walk last week,
that is where

the red racer crossed your path
just yesterday. *Be present*.
Notice the ants

mining their kingdom underground.
The angel dissipates
only to reappear as rain.

My Father's War

—for Henry David Esau (1913-1997)

Life is perfect.
My father is five years old,
youngest son of a Mennonite pastor
in this quiet Ukrainian village.

This is before the Revolution.
Before the wounded soldiers appear at the door.
Before the children start finding bodies in the field.
Before the family is reduced to eating garbage.
Before the Bolsheviks march their horses
like shining toys across the Steppes.

Before the family flees by train to Estonia,
by boat to England, by ship to Canada.
Before they become outsiders in a Protestant land.
Long before World War II, when my father joins
the RCAF, trains airmen who take off and never return,
gets reassigned to a German POW camp in Alberta,
exchanges drawings, jokes and smokes
with prisoners just as lost as he.

This is before I am born.

It is a perfect day,
a cloudless, windless, summer day.
Everyone at work in the fields, the kitchens,
the barns. Amid the gentle sounds of their labors,
a distant buzz like a mosquito in the next room.
Then a biplane, weaving its way erratically
above the squares of rye and wheat,
banking over the schoolhouse and church,

21

circling the cows grazing in the paddock,
casting a shadow like a giant hawk.
Now they see the pilot, flying low, flying crazy,
goggles askew, scaring the chickens and ducks,
setting the dogs barking, stopping the workers
in mid-task, steering with one gloved hand,
reaching inside the cockpit with the other,
pulling something up, holding something out,
dropping something down, watching something fall
toward the herd, explode like thunder at their feet,
send smoke and sod and pieces of cow
like fireworks spiraling through the morning air,
the biplane arcing, jerking, diving like a rabid bird
of prey, the pilot reaching again inside his cockpit,
holding out again that instrument of death,
dropping again that terrible bomb, reaching,
holding, dropping, watching again and again
and again until the detonations stop, the air stills,
the mouths close, the tears spill, till every last cow
lies shattered as the morning calm.

Some say they heard the pilot laugh
as he banked and sputtered away
like a hacking drunk back from where he came.

Life is perfect.
My father is dead, years after quitting booze,
leaving wives and children, abandoning art

and giving up on life. It simply made no sense
to him, the death, the insanity, the slaughter
of innocents on the golden fields of his youth.

He never forgot the cows,
couldn't shake the specter of that drunken bomber,
couldn't abide that shell-shocked exit from childhood.
For my father stood among the herd that day,
did not survive beyond the perfect age of five.

Aground

The rest of the fishers in the Southeast fleet
drop their nets in semi-circles amid
the swirling kelp beds all around him.
Holding strong against the minus tide,
they watch from flying bridges and skiffs
for jumpers and finners before they close
their sets, lift rings and leadlines
through power blocks overhead,
pile their corks and web while rolling
on the ocean swells, haul in humpies
and kings by the brailerload.
All the seiners in this jigsaw jumble
of vicious competition, fighting to fill their
holds while the fish run and the feds allow —

except him, the highliner from Juneau,
looking on with his crew from the afterdeck
of the Coast Guard tug *Victory*, helpless
while his precious *Jenny Jo* perches
atop a cradle of rocks, listing like a derelict
to starboard, straining hard against the ropes.
Her red wood hull sits a good two fathoms
out of the sea, vulnerable as a starfish
on the sand, exposed like the ivory-white
back of the skipper as he stands, shirtless,
smoking yet another Marlboro
in the rare Alaskan heat, waiting for the moon
to move, in control of nothing until the flood.

Loretta's Sacred Mission

Christ told Loretta during prayer one day to convert
the old double-wide to a writers retreat, renovate
the back bedroom where the grandkids made a mess
with their chemistry set, replace the flood-stained carpeting,
fix the well pump, rebuild the utility porch
once they exterminated the termites — and paint it purple,
inside and out. Plant peonies and lilies to beautify
the borders. Put frills on the windows, flowers on the sills,
baskets on the walls. Place a Bible by the Holstein figurines
on the dinette shelves, complimentary homemade jam
and muffins on the counter by the stove. Make it Heavenly,

He said. Inspire them and their higher natures.
Let them come here to write their words and leave here
to spread The Word. Let their hearts be filled with the glory
of this high plateau just miles as a crow flies
from what you call "Mesa Verd": the yearlings munching
spring grass beyond the electric fence, the tireless pumping
of gas wells, the majesty of mountains and purity of air,
the honesty of labor and sanctity of soil, the meadowlarks
and red-winged blackbirds singing praise songs
from the plane trees and telephone wires.
The Lord has made you His shepherdess, Loretta,
has graced you with dominion over flocks and fields,
has charged you and Luke with bringing His fallen seeds
to fruition. Now it is up to you to make this vision manifest.

Let them be reborn in your garden, Loretta, baptized
in your bathtub, inspired at your granddad's walnut writing
desk. Let them tell their published friends: This is holy
pastureland. This is God's Country. This is where Jesus
himself would live if he were a poet today.

This is your mission, Loretta — after you milk the cows
and mow the lawn, muck out the barn and put up
some rhubarb, feed the chickens and cook for your man.
Believe in yourself as you believe in the Lord, Loretta,
and someday you, too, will witness your own name in print.

Things Fall Apart

— after William Butler Yeats (1865-1939)

The roof is leaking again, I tell
my daughter by email, dripping
like a ticking clock from *vigas*
in the den, dropping on curtains,
tables, chairs. It started when snowmelt
froze, blocked *canales* last week.

Yesterday, when temperatures again
topped forty, I climbed back up, tarred
the cracks in the flashing, along
the rooftop, around downspouts, then
hoped our indoor rainstorm was done.

Last night, though, a front moved in
from Utah, left six more inches
of snow. When the sun burned bright
today, crystals turned to slush, puddled,
seeped through the ceiling once again.

Yeats was right: things fall apart.
Our sliding doors stick in their tracks,
the chimney plaster is cracked,
needs to be restuccoed this year.
The garage door shudders and jerks,
our woodwork is scratched, carpets
stained by animals, fences warped.

My daughter is studying in Belfast
this semester, learning from experts
how to mediate anarchy loosed
upon the world. She knows how it feels

when the center does not hold, when
Dad is thousands of miles away,
when darkness drops and he's not there
to read her to sleep. But she is growing
up fast, grasping at last how ceremonies
of innocence get drowned.

It happens all around us, not just in times
of war or revelation. Glaciers crumble.
Oceans rise. Jungles get reduced
to stubble. Prairies buried under miles
of steel and concrete.

I'll pay someone to do our roof if I have to.
I'll buy new doors, try to patch the adobe
and fence as best I can. But who will fix
the world? What force will dam
the blood-dimmed tide, its hour
come round at last?

We'll use our pots and pans to save us
from this flood; we have no vessel
wide enough to catch the falling sky.

High Desert Monsoon

Let the wind rip the last remaining leaves
off the cottonwood trees, the rainwater
surge like a tsunami down the arroyo.

We have coffee served in our favorite mugs,
mine with brandy, yours with chocolate.
We have Schubert on the stereo.

You sign Christmas cards at your desk,
address and seal the envelopes.
I write this poem sitting up in bed.

We have flannel sheets, cinnamon rolls,
candles scented with sandalwood.
The animals are all asleep. Let me sing

my gratitude for the roof over our heads,
the radiant heat underfoot, the comfort
of this home we have made together.

May you hear the silent call of my desire,
let your robe fall to the hardwood floor.
Let us celebrate another day of staying alive.

This is how we shelter in the storm.
This is how we remember the ocean left behind.
This is how we keep each other dry.

The Human Scale

Somewhere between the Very Large Array
and Biosphere 2, we rediscovered
the human scale of our relationship.
Radio wave echoes from the Big Bang
cannot start a conversation about
the origins of our intimacy,
and all the microclimates in the world
never will engender reciprocity.

But, after the VLA gift shop closed
and before we decided not to tour
the glassed-in artificial atmosphere,
along about the time our RV stalled,
we realized that life makes perfect sense
over cold beer by the side of the road.

Truck Stop Theory

To prove your premise that trucker cafes
do not in fact offer the very finest
in late-night cuisine along the interstate,
you pull our compact rental rig up
at Travelers Oasis, its gaudy neon display
promising "America's Best Truck Stop."

We peruse souvenir jackalope coffee mugs,
imitation turquoise-inlaid pocketknives
and Hell's Canyon shot glasses, then slide
into a frayed vinyl booth, its tar-stained
ashtrays half-filled with Marlboro butts,
its table tent touting Bud Lite. Our waitress
for the evening is Jackie, who actually pops
her gum and calls us "hon." You order
chicken-fried steak and fries, I risk
the Fettuccini Alfredo chef's special,
get a pile of congealed noodles
bigger than my head. We forego dessert.

"See?" you gloat, then saunter off to buy
your wife a miniature personalized Idaho
license plate while I, in mute acceptance
of the irrefutable truth, step outside
for a breath of diesel smoke before taking
the wheel and heading on down the pike
for Mountain Home.

College Girls Dig Jazz

When my big brother Jim quit
junior college for basic training
in Texas I was into early Beatles.
He said college girls dig Brubeck.

He bought a Chevy Impala ragtop
long low and sleek with flying fins
two-tone aqua Naugahyde interior
dual exhausts dual rear antennas.

He said they think it's sexy except
he wrecked it driving home from
Rapid City in the snow. Before he
shipped out he showed me his secret

Polaroids: Him and some pimply guy
chugging Buds, the crumpled front end
of his Impala, a blonde in her girdle
and bra. He said college girls *love* jazz.

Thirst

He wonders if his narrative is rich enough, if twenty years
of reservation life can weave like raw wool the weft of story,
if his desperate teenage episode can hold his readers rapt
as turkey vultures gyring the still-warm hulk of a fallen elk.

Ten red hours since my grandma banged her frying pan
on the iron stove to wake me, since I gulped my bacon
and eggs, gripped my pack and stick and left the Hogan,
led our sheep and goats out the gate and down the trail.

He's learned the terms for image, symbol, metaphor, but
can't get past the syntax of this incident that shaped his
adolescence, the white man's grammar cinching his words
the way his down-heeled cowboy boots once pinched his toes.

I'm crouching in the scanty shade of tamarisk, the tracks
in sienna sand proof our thirsty herd had strayed this way.
Six hours since my tin canteen ran dry, since my throat
began to parch like the bark of a withered cottonwood.

He knew this arroyo from drives with his uncle,
he explains, but can't describe that wide, dry scar
that ambled like a stagger west across the line
from Navajo land, can't find words for those final,
searing hours of cracked lips and cramping thighs,
that numbing desire for sleep.

The passing herd sucked every puddle dry. Vultures
coil into a listless funnel cloud, and now this shimmer
of ribs picked clean as earthenware. But there — beyond
that brittlebush — a roil of dust...a rumble up the wash....

Song for Rahim Alhaj

Chords like cries from rubble
his head bent over his oud

he cradles her in his lap
her carved neck angled back

strums like breath
plays the light back into the moon

wind rustles dry leaves
tears fall like shooting stars

embers in the night
he carries his mother in his eyes

smoke disguising clouds
cousins murdered at taxi stands

first song he ever heard
last song his mother sang

Iraqi lullaby
he cradles her in his lap

Evening Prayer

The Imam sings from his minaret,
calls out to his followers in the slums

around the two-star Jakarta hotel.
In my room, I bow to the East,

to the West, to the open window.
Smell of diesel smoke and cloves.

Virga

Clouds like a torn curtain
hanging over the mountains
A boy waits for his father's return

Raindrops turn to ice crystals
evaporate in mid-air
A mortar detonates near Baghdad

The boy stands mute
clutching a folded flag
Some rain never reaches the ground

Trial by Canoe

After the whale calf nibbled the bow of their canoe
she knew it was a bad idea

climbing in a birch-bark boat with her betrothed
paddling all the way around the island

battling riptides and broadside waves
freighter wakes and sideways rain

The elders said it was a way to learn
called it spirit time   not human time

time to trust the wisdom of the ceremony
time to put their wedding date on hold

Still it didn't make this test the best way
to calm her terror of the open sea

From the time they shoved off from shore
he yelled at her all day to keep up with his pace

called her useless as a reservation dog
worst of all he told her she was weak

At sunset they returned   more or less intact
except for wedding plans thrown overboard.

That night she smiled in her blanket by the fire
knowing she could paddle on her own

II.

Thrashers

Each arriving bird carries
a necessary piece of spring —

conical buds bursting through
twigs of trees, sinewy blooms
gathering strength to pierce
the mulch and frozen dirt —

even the rising sun, earlier
by minutes every day,
borne on wings of birds
across the thawing sky
one increment at a time.

There — in that *cholla* —
a pair of curve-billed thrashers
weaving this year's nest.

Ingénue

She lets one strap of her cotton dress slip
from her shoulder to reveal a glimpse
of crocuses poking through the snow,

spins to the rhythm of wind chimes,
mimics the curve of raised beds,
the blush of a waking tulip bulb.

Her gaze is the color of sky, her hair
wild reeds inviting redwinged blackbirds
to weave their nests, whistle their songs.

Beneath her hem a flash of blooming stalks
and flowering shrub, a scent that intoxicates
honeybees, drives young trumpeter swans

to beat their wings on the surface of the lake.
Her white-haired father, with his icicle beard
and glacial eyes, tries to stop her wanton

display, scolds, rebuffs, but soon resigns
himself to this rite of passage and crawls
back to sleep in his cave of ice.

Planting in May

Alice is outside planting a clematis for Mother's Day.
She thinks it might be too soon, but she wants to honor
her sister who died last month of the same genetic disease
she has, who helped raise her because their mother
for the last twelve years of her life was in a wheelchair,
an insane asylum, or both.

It's been cold lately, especially at night. The tulips have come
and gone, lilacs already starting to fade. Still, it could freeze
one more time or even snow in this harsh high desert.
It isn't like Missouri, where the girls planted nasturtiums
every spring simply by scattering seeds at random in the dark
river soil of their back yard, where cherries and pecans
flourished on trees no one ever bothered to prune.

Here the ground is all sand and clay, water scarce,
the sun unforgiving as their small town priest.
Here Alice lays to rest the memory of those women
who taught her to love the fertile earth, despite the injustice
of it all. Here she learns to put things in pots, not trust
to the vagaries of climate and drought.

Alice is a master gardener. She knows all about pests,
xeriscaping, compost bins. This clematis start will root,
will join the lavender, roses and thyme she's placed just so
around the patio and out beyond the fence beside
the wild sage. It might snow tonight, Alice knows, noticing
the lenticular clouds forming around the peaks
of the Sangre de Cristo. Still, she builds a trellis
out of thin bamboo to support the vines as they wind
their way toward the heat and light. It might be too soon.

Placenta

You walked across town in nothing
but a blanket. That was the morning after
they released you from solitary confinement.
That was the bottom.

Pissing yourself in the cell.
Hallucinating slits on your wrists, becoming the face
of Jesus. Having to be pronounced sane
by a colleague at the clinic. The knowledge
of the depth of your addictions.

That was the day before you quit booze,
joined AA, flushed your pot down the john.
Before your boss gave you a month
of mandatory R&R, the acupuncturist
prescribed cleansing herbs, the shaman smudged
your house. Before your ex-wife and children,
your brothers, sisters and friends formed a circle
around you, let you fall where you would.

You're still falling. Weightless, certain you'll be caught,
held, healed. There will be time to lie in the sun
by the cottonwood that grows where you buried
the placenta of your son, where you plant the memories
of a life half-lived.

Bottle Tree

Mirabelle recalls too well the moans
of evil spirits whistling on the river wind
evaporating in the Delta dawn

She dreams of cobalt blue bottles
stuck upside down on crepe myrtle trees
outside the Creole tenements of her youth

hears the Hoodoo cries of genies
trapped at night by encircling charms

imagines her grandmama cork them up
throw them in the great Congo River
watch them as they wash away

In the hollow of her bones
immobile as the half-spent fifth of gin
standing right-side-up on the orange crate
beside her threadbare daybed

somewhere between heaven and earth
Mirabelle knows her own blue soul hangs
in the balance

begs in this involuntary sleep
to be created or destroyed

Calla Lilies

Sun is out   stars in hiding
Let this be a metaphor
for the mystery we praise

Our neighbor died yesterday
on the day she turned eighty-nine
We didn't have a chance
to say our goodbyes

Last night you placed your palm
on the small of my back
and the pain subsided
We've gardens to sow   to tend

We do our watering by the moon
You paint a chrysanthemum
from memory   I saw a canyon towhee
to add to my life list

You and I are twins   mirrors
The calla lilies on their elegant stalks
promise to unfurl

Sunday Paper

I look for eagles
as I walk along the road.
It is a long road.

I'm bringing back the Sunday paper
from the Mount Erie Grocery.
A cold wind has kicked up

from the southeast.
I'm walking into the wind,
grateful for Gortex and wool.

It's a colder wind than last week,
carrying the taste of snow
down from the Cascades.

Clouds rush past other clouds
like sheep running in a field.
Wood smoke, bluer than the clouds,

blows sideways from the farmhouse
chimneys along the way.
Several trees lie fallen

from last week's storm.
I watch for eagles
circling the mountain,

or lower, over the pastures
bordering Campbell Lake.
A dog barks.

A calf grazes by a cow.
A lone Canada goose flies south.
Four robins chase a crow.

I head up the long, gravel driveway
to our house, past the rooster,
the mule, ducks, geese.

It isn't until I'm back inside,
reading the paper by the wood stove,
that I see them through the window:

two bald eagles, riding the currents
of the wind, black against the sky
like headlines over the world.

Sha-Sha Says

Sha-Sha says you're sick
don't have right thinking
don't know you are center
of universe
universe is center of you

Sha-Sha was there
at Tiananmen Square
survived the interrogation
married an American
has two American boys

Sha-Sha says your cells
not make fresh all time
need new information
need spirit body physical body
same body

Sha-Sha is an Aires dragon
double trouble she says
party girl philosopher
knows the answer
to your problem

Right thinking make cells
fresh all time she says
not kill cancer
love cancer
make cancer whole again

And you who danced
with your friend in the streets
of Beijing drank till you spoke
a common tongue
you with your mind in a vice

And your ovaries at war
what do you think?
Still a wild woman you say
still double trouble
still make fresh all time.

Home by Dark

— *after a photograph by Eudora Welty (1909-2001)*

She turns around to look
that black woman on the back of the horse-drawn cart
on the flat dirt road disappearing into the sun

turning back to look at what might be gaining on her
as she rides into the sun
what might be gathering in the shadows

every emotion waiting on her gesture
waiting on that backwards glance of longing curiosity fear
hostage to the pace of the horse

to the sauntering pace of desegregation
to the blinding pace of her life
as she rides not drives that cart into the setting sun

afraid to look ahead at the solitary magnolia tree on the left
the strange fruit tree   afraid to look ahead
unable to look away

Inclination

She tilts her head when she turns to talk
or looks the other way, executes
that nearly imperceptible lean and toss
to swing her hip-length tresses clear

of her shoulders, earrings, chair back.
She's a survivor whose singular trait
since girlhood has been to care for her hair
as though it were the very golden heart of her.

Now wrapped in a pink silk scarf,
she still inclines her head to turn, performs
that customary self-protective demi-circle,
throws her phantom locks free from harm.

Wandering the Women's Exhibit

Everything is made of something else
acrylic moon   latex stamen
paper wedding assemblage
Nothing is as it seems

Those koi are only oil on canvas
That mesa merely charcoal

I wander this women's exhibit
in search of   what?   Myself?
Parts of myself? Tints   shades
shapes   perspective?

Here's a floor projection of a dancer
spinning in forest light
There's a fabricated metal kimono
beyond a woodcut cowboy shirt

What's a person to make of this display?
Where does my spittle and sputum fit in
my white cells   gray matter   blue eyes
flesh flesh?

War shirt of human hair   Limbo in clay
woodblock polkadot apron   It matters

Matter matters
no matter how it is arranged
my ceramic heart   cardboard spleen
cast iron intestinal tract

I sculpt myself   bake myself
in an old adobe kiln   extract   extrude
explain myself in tempera on paper
oil on linen   stone on stone

I love the steel flock   the plastic thread
of Ocotillo Dust Devil
the watercolored Red High Heels
the woven Awakening

There's more to do than wander
more to be than voyeur
more to have than vision
Let me simply spin   in light

Portrait

All the art in the world
is not hung on this wall

this empty space

in which one eye
does not behold another

shadow
falling on shadow

all the paint
the paper
the canvas

unused

The moon rose tonight
less than full

again

I could not see her face

The one with violets in her lap

— after Sappho (630?-520? BCE)

the one whose hem slips up to her hips
as she shifts in her wicker seat

the one with finch crown cheeks
and fingers tightened on a broken stick

biting her lip
tea grown tepid

the one who notices cracks in the plaster
smells the neighbor's new-turned soil

whose socks hang on her chairback
feet rest atop her clogs

the one shivering in her sundress
humming a fragment of song

spies a bicycle in the distance
lets her thighs   just   unclench

The Little Store

The canned peas display stack
makes a perfect pyramid by the front door.
I've restocked all the cigarette packs
on the rack above the cash register.
The ice chest is filled with Coke bottles,
Hires, Nehi, Orange Crush. The floor is swept.
No one at the gas pumps.

Through the backwards lettering on the window
facing the street, I see that light green Packard
pass by, turn in to the second driveway on the left.
They've had that same car for twelve years;
the mother's dress is easily half that old.
The boy collects empties from the ditch
on weekends, redeems them for milk or bread.

The mother opens the trunk, glances my way
to see if I'm looking, has the boy lift the paper bags
and hurriedly carry them in the back door.
She looks again, shuts the trunk, scurries inside.

I feel her shame from here, can almost see
the crimson of her cheeks, the worried hunch
of her shoulders. She owes me money,
sends her boy for two or three items at a time —
eggs, thread, oatmeal, Winston filters.
She never comes in herself.

I know she goes to the supermarket to stock up
on canned goods, potatoes, TV dinners,
budget cuts of meat. They have better prices,
bigger selection, fresher produce. I know that.

What she doesn't know is that it's okay.
I don't care if she shops at the new Safeway
or if she ever pays her account in full.
What she doesn't know is I'd let her
and her boy shop here free for life if I could,
if my wife would let me. What she doesn't know
is she's lovely in her old dress, her used car,
her run-down house. I wish I could —

but here's a paying customer at the pump.
He drives a brand new Pontiac Grand Prix.
He owns the new split-level on the hill,
works for a mortgage insurance company.
He honks. He wears a suit and tie,
never gets out of his car.
Will that be regular or ethyl?

Garden Shed

There's nothing growing in the garden shed
this May — just rusting shovels, rakes and hoes.
He sleeps alone now in their double bed.

He should be planning for the months ahead
and planting seeds by now, I would suppose,
though nothing's growing in the garden shed

he built for her the summer they were wed.
That winter they stayed warm, despite the snow,
but he's alone now in their double bed.

He wakes alone, gets dressed, somehow gets fed
and stumbles through the day — that's how it goes
when nothing's growing in the garden shed,

when no one's there to tell him how to spread
the manure or where to dump the compost
bin. He sleeps alone in their double bed

this year, for all the years that lie ahead.
They say a man will reap just what he sows,
but nothing's growing in the garden shed,
and he's alone now in their double bed.

The Pink Umbrella

— after a print by Nicholas Verrall

Three blue chairs and a bench
sit on a patio beneath a pink umbrella
with white stripes, slightly askew.

Yellow serving tray on wood-slat table,
black coffee pot by glass of milk,
cups and saucers, butter, toast, juice.

Mid-morning. Light from the side,
shadows lean on a wooden fence,
thicket beyond, birch leaves just turning

to gold. But what of the couple
who will breakfast by these woods?
Perhaps they are on vacation, not yet risen

from beneath their comforter. Perhaps
they practice lingering, listening in bed
for the flicker and chickadee before

venturing barefoot across the puzzle
of fallen leaves forming on stones. Smell
of eggs and bacon, damp grass, maple smoke.

Reed Flute

I am the drum
the gong
a gourd filled with seed
a reed flute
a ram's horn
sticks beaten together
a click of the tongue

I hear her climb the stairs
turn the key in the lock
open and close her door
drop her boots on the floor
open and close
a dresser drawer
bang on the drainpipe
like a gamelan

I am a trance
a dance
a thrum in the throat
a chant like a prayer flag
flapping in the breeze

I never see her
in the stairwell
at the mailbox
down the street
at the delicatessen
have no clue who she is
what she looks like
why the jangle of her life
underscores my quietude

Outside the rain taps
the windowglass
like tiny timpani
buses hum past
splashing *shush-sh*
a fire truck rumbles by
siren piercing the night

and here am I
in my stockinged feet
dancing on old linoleum
to the Godfather of Soul
trying to conjure
at least the sound of her voice.

III.

Back When I Used to be White

— after Mark Turcotte

1.
I am digging a hip-high pit
in the shovel-clump soil
of the Little Woods
felling thigh-thick birch
snipping cedar boughs
to thatch our pit-house roof
we three neighbor boys
the only braves
in the Indian Club
whittling spears sharpening arrows
bending sapling bows with kite string
setting traps for cottontails
dams for brook trout
tin-can strands across trails
to warn us of enemies
or parents in the dark
trekking into the Doug fir forest
bare-chested in the August heat
hand-towel loincloths
tucked into belts over bluejeans
ripped up strips of pillowcase
tied around our heads
sneaking through gullies of mud
speaking in our secret tongue
creeping through the sword fern
devil's club heavy-nettle underbrush
returning from our hunt at dusk
as bats begin to slice the air
empty-handed slump-shouldered
hungry weary wet

back in the flicker-dark
of our tribal fort
back into pjs tube socks
J.C. Penney moccasins
sleeping bags and pillows spread
on tarps across the hard-dirt floor
telling tales of bravery
laughing at danger
happy for Kool-Aid
Wonder Bread
and Sunny Jim peanut butter.

2.
I am standing in the back field
aiming my birthday BB gun
at a chipping sparrow
in the apple tree overhead
aiming squeezing firing
watching as it doesn't even try
to fly
just falls like rotten fruit
in the grass at my feet
and it's not till my big brother
yells at me
tells me I shouldn't shoot
an innocent bird
that I look back up
at where it used to be.

3.
I am toweling off
in the locker room after P.E.
a sixty-pound seventh-grader
thin as balsawood
pale as a tetherball
when my tall friend Larry
the only Indian in class
grabs me for no known reason
slams me against the wall
hurt and hatred scrawled
like hieroglyphics across his face
tears bleeding from his eyes
as he throws me to the floor
and bursts out the door
to the antiseptic smell
of the hall.

4.
I am circling the mat
looking for an opening
against a freshman wrestler
from the rez across the bay
a Lummi boy with fear
like fireworks in his eyes
circling feigning seeking
that awkward cross-step moment
ducking under his futile guard
executing a textbook takedown
spilling him flat
on his coffee-colored back
pinning him in record time

one   and two   and three!
the referee slaps the mat
the cheer girls kick their legs
clap their hands jump up and down
in their sacred Red & White uniforms
chant in unison *Here we go*
Red Raiders, Here we go!
as my arm is raised in victory
and all I can think of in the din
is driving to Herfy's afterwards
in my tricked-out Pontiac Super Chief
for a cheeseburger and vanilla shake.

A Face in the Ice

Just a thin, frozen puddle in the parking lot
of an abandoned fish cannery by the harbor —

it figures our stepfather would take us there,
near the wharf where his troller was moored.
He was most at ease by the bay, near his web locker
and What's the Catch Café. Like other old Norskis,
he bought his black coffee there every morning,
swapped news and Swede jokes with skippers and mates,
listened for gale warnings, hot leads on used gear.

Maybe that's how he got the skates. It surprised us,
him driving us to the accidental rink with tin cans,
pint bottles, crab pots sealed into its surface like lumps
in our morning mush. It wasn't a real rink —
but then he wasn't a real dad, never took us camping
like Mr. McLeod next door, couldn't throw a football,
hated Elvis.

But there he was, helping us with our laces,
demonstrating how to turn and glide and stop, carving
up the ice like Bobby Orr, wielding his stick
like the ringer he'd been at pickup games in Norma,
North Dakota. He even laughed once after slapping
the cork float puck through my brother's legs,
raised his tattooed arms in triumph and let loose
a startling falsetto yip like a slipping fan belt
on the old John Deere back at the family farm.

Under the ice, watching us teeter and spill like clowns,
he sees the face of an old Norwegian, disapproving.

Flicker in the Cottonwood

You are a bird with a voice
Every egg forms in your soul
You cannot sing yesterday
Autumn is the time to plant trees

Every egg forms in your soul
For mulch we use fallen leaves
Autumn is the time to plant trees
Today you visit the nursery

For mulch we use fallen leaves
Together we'll dig the holes
Today you visit the nursery
Mugo pines will grow by our path

Together we'll dig the holes
We fill the birdbath with rainwater
Mugo pines will grow by our path
I heard the first flicker in the cottonwood

We fill the birdbath with rainwater
In the sun our laundry dries
I heard the first flicker in the cottonwood
Tonight we'll light a juniper fire

Tonight we'll read to each other
You are a bird with a voice
The linden trees are nearly naked
You cannot sing yesterday

Leap, Float

—for Robert Ewart Sarvis (1924-2011)

In the spotlight of this day, the heat should heal,
untwist the knot of my spine. But darkness bunches
there, below the scrim of skin. *What is here?*
And what is gone?

The fine, strong man. The bright look, resonant
laugh. *How I wanted what he was, what they had:*
steadfast husband, father. Ski trips, waterfront
property. What lies beyond.

He even died right: a shaft of sunlight falling
on his face just as he released himself, from himself.
His steady wife. Their strong, fine sons. *So much*
to envy and to praise.

A three-point buck bursts through a border
of reeds, crosses the grass, suspended like a dancer
above the stage — leaping, floating, leaping again.
Do I touch the ground? Do I dare?

Bark Beetles

These runic lines
engraved on this thumb
of ponderosa pine —

a pattern of loss.
Useless thunder clouds,
tears like virga.

Eighth grade metal shop,
my sleeve catches on a lathe.
I am unscathed

but my sweater is ruined,
my only sweater.
Someone steals my bike,

makes me walk to school,
no money for another bike.
Someone takes my dad.

Desert wind strips the bark,
reveals the insects' handiwork.
Let this be good enough.

Squash Bugs

Watering my plot in the late-day heat,
I pick through the twist of stems and stalks
for the thieves of my crookneck yield.

Squash bugs are breaking through the lines
of diatomaceous earth, sucking the life
from my zucchini vines, planting clusters
of eggs under succulent pumpkin leaves.

I have a choice here: crush the nymphs
between my finger and thumb, drown them
in an admix of bleach or let them survive
to blight my crop. It always comes to this.

Chokeberries retake the slope where the mud
slide flowed. Wildfires free seeds from cones.
Someone will work this earth when we're gone.

A Morning in the Sun

The sun in its lazy January arc
can't outshine the gathering storm
tumbling down from the mountains.

Flurries are forecast for today, they say,
and maybe tomorrow, as well.
What do we expect, we who choose
to winter in this Land of Enchantment?
We're here because of the sunlight —
we can handle a bit more snow.

We've still got some wood left
in a pile by the patio, the heat
of juniper and sweetness of pinon.
It's a good combination.

We're a good combination —
me with my bright denial,
you with your faith in change.
I chose you and your predestination,
you accepted my history of grief.

How many more of these Sundays
will we share like this,
reading and writing by the fire,
blind to our dwindling supply
of heat and light? Do we really care?

The first few flakes have started to fall.
We'll walk the dogs while we can,
I'll shovel the steps when we return.

There's plenty of food in the fridge.
Let the ash-gray sky drape us
like a shroud, keep us home
from errands and work.

At this point, we can't be picky,
we'll take what weather we are sent —
a morning in the sun,
an afternoon of turbulent white,
preparation for the night.

Terroir

What is the taste of earth
if not the tongue extended

to catch the rain before it drops
anonymous into Puget Sound

garden knees stained by clay
gloves with holes in the thumbs

you spend summers picking specks of dirt
off strawberries between rows

so you can bake a home-made pie
for your man at the end of the day

you remember that packet of squash seeds
lost for years behind the workbench

you feed the worms your table scraps
and use their castings as compost

your shovel crusted with last week's mud
sweat stains on your favorite hat

you inhale the iodine and salt
from the morning tide

yet all you can smell is black cherries
dark coffee a hint of oak

ripe plums dropping like rose petals

Cold Mountain

Han-shan says after a moment of bliss,
this is better than where I live. I see
Cold Mountain disappearing into mist,

my life among these thousand-meter cliffs,
my days of hermitage and poverty
evanescing in a moment of bliss.

I look in the mirror and I see wisps
of white, like clouds among the leafless trees,
Cold Mountain disappearing into mist.

This day and the years gone by are mindless
ripples, like rivers flowing to the east —
Han-shan vanishing on moments of bliss.

I have no desire now to reminisce
about my profession or family
as Cold Mountain disappears into mist.

Some may ask, did Han-shan ever exist?
Yes, I did, but now I have been set free —
a puff of smoke in a moment of bliss,
Cold Mountain disappearing into mist....

Carrizozo Waitress

The waitress apologizes, says she's too young
to serve us beer, too uncoordinated to carry
two plates at a time so she can't serve us
all at once, doesn't smile because she wears braces.

This is Tammy's first time in the dining room.
Normally she cooks, washes dishes,
carries out the trash. She's been too busy
to clean the restrooms. She apologizes for that,

and for the Mexican Combo, which she thinks
is overdone. She wouldn't have cooked it so much,
she tells us as she refills our water glasses —
over the floor because she's afraid she'll spill
on the table. Because she's so uncoordinated.

By the time we decline the coconut layer cake
and choice of homemade pie, Tammy has told us
all about her miniature Schnauzer named Fuzzy,
the quarter horse she had to put down last year,
and her boyfriend Ryan who dumped her.
Because of the braces. She smiles anyway.

Girl on the Bridge

Hot day in the gray Northwest, ebb tide boiling
like crab water two hundred feet below Deception
Pass Bridge, busloads of Chinese tourists clicking
photos of granite cliffs, twisted madrona trees.

A teenage blond in shorts and halter top leans
over the rail, clears her throat and lobs a great gob
of spit, watches it disperse before it hits
the blue-green swirl. Later

the tide goes slack, lapping waves begin to retake
sandbars, matted seaweed rises again in tidal pools,
sandpipers scurry on reed-thin legs, pursue
hermit crabs. A great blue heron flaps by, neck
tucked, legs trailing like streamers in the wind.
A red-tail hawk watches for cottontails
among the dune grass.

I like the spitting image of that girl, leaning
over the void, testing her power.

Play of Light

I've intercepted the light
in its downward fall.
It would have fallen anyway,
but it would have landed
somewhere else.

I've moved, and the play
of light has changed, bent,
shifted the shadows
that slant below me.

I did this without effort —
I simply raised my hand,
gestured, lowered my hand.

I've deflected something,
part of myself perhaps,
onto someone else,
you perhaps.

Perhaps you've changed.
Perhaps you raise your hand,
gesture in return.

I close my eyes —
you're still there.

Moths

It got hot
just like that

a squadron of moths
from nowhere

like little MiGs
divebomb the floodlight

on the back deck
bang their soft heads

against the candent bulb
thud into the sliding door

leave fine brown dust
where they collide

propel their fuselage bodies
in a frenzy that belies

the invisible smile
on the crescent moon

as it brushes past
Venus

Grandfather

The moon is pregnant
I'm too old to be a father
staying up nights to count new stars

Ice looks just like water
on the asphalt looks like night
the dark blanket holding in the cold

I almost fell three times
walking the dog this afternoon
the gaudy glisten of snow

like sequins on a strapless gown
dazzling even through sunglasses
There goes a child on a sled

scraping down the empty street
not my child just someone
faster than I younger than my dog

I take no responsibility for this freeze
blame it on the solstice
I'll sleep in a cave tonight

dreaming of that face on the moon
that sly smile that teases the tides
induces grown men to howl

I will not strike tinder to flint
nor try to spark a darkened sky
I will help come up with a name

Granddaughter

—for Luisa Anna

It won't always be this way
this first ferocious gulp
each flail of your dimpled arms
a clamorous grab for surface

For you in your uncurling
each suck will bring purchase
you will not scream yourself mute
nor die of dirty pants

Your burble will be deciphered
In time you will unriddle
the womb beyond the womb
name those hands that rough and choke

decode the cooing of scavengers
The sky will fill with falling leaves
the earth enfold you in its crib
Your trust is to remember

Artificial Tree

Morning light shines high
on the kitchen wall as the sun
rides low in the southern sky.

Last night we took our tree
out of the box, unfolded its branches,
stood it near the fireplace.
Today it glistens with lights,
garlands, glass balls, an angel
playing a violin.

I just made more coffee,
served Alice a cup in bed.
She's not feeling well again.

I'm putting off going to work
because there isn't much work to do.
But at least my business
is still in business,
and Alice can still walk.

We could fail to notice the frost
on the fence or the way
the linden branches dance in the breeze.

We could have taken a walk
in the forest to find the perfect pine,
sawed it down, dragged it
through the snow, hauled it home.

But pitch is so hard
to wash off one's hands.
And the planet is dying.

The cats are stretched out
on the bed with Alice.
The telephone rings in my office
down the hall.
Sunlight makes a halo
on the angel as she plays.

White Glass

It is that
which generally
gets ignored —

the plain, the
pale, the subtle —
always there,

available —
those unclaimed
fragments of glass

orphaned on the strand,
the ones the tide
unmothers,

those pieces unseen
by passers-by,
dullards

of the diamond clan.
These are the gifts
for the modest,

these partners of sand,
this union of substance
and light.

Swimming Through Space

I'm swimming through space
warmed by the sun

cooled by the sea

reaching first with one arm
then the other

breathing every second reach

beating my legs
three kicks per stroke

letting my feet relax

finding my rhythm
setting a tireless pace

propelled by breath
and buoyed by my desire

to touch the farthest shore

then keep on crawling
till I reach the stars

About the Author

Born in Abbotsford, B.C., to a Ukrainian/Canadian father and a Canadian/American mother, Wayne Lee (wayneleepoet.com) was raised in Bellingham, Washington, where he earned his B.A. in English and M.A. in Theatre/Dance from Western Washington University. He has worked as a commercial fisherman, actor/dancer, teacher, journalist, public information officer, and owner of a tutoring company.

Lee won the 2012 Mark Fischer Poetry Prize and the SICA Poems for Peace Prize, and has been nominated for a Pushcart Prize and three Best of the Net awards. His previous poetry collections include *Doggerel & Caterwauls: Poems Inspired by Cats & Dogs* (Red Mountain Press), and *Twenty Poems from the Blue House* (with Alice Lee, Whistle Lake Press).

Lee lives with his wife, poet/painter Alice Lee, and their golden retriever Austin in Santa Fe, New Mexico, where he works as an editor, educator and wedding officiant. They have three daughters (Mica, Annie and Molly) and two granddaughters (Luisa and Emma).